The Wonder of Love

Books edited by Phyllis Hobe
Published by The Westminster Press

The Wonder of Love
The Wonder of Prayer
The Wonder of Comfort

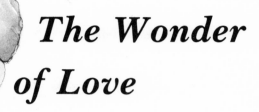

The Wonder of Love

**Edited by
Phyllis Hobe**

*Drawings by
Jennifer Cole*

**Bridgebooks
Philadelphia**

Book Design by Alice Derr

First edition

Bridgebooks
Published by The Westminster Press®
Philadelphia, Pennsylvania

PRINTED IN THE UNITED STATES OF AMERICA
9 8 7 6 5 4 3 2 1

Library of Congress Cataloging in Publication Data

Main entry under title:

The Wonder of love.

   Includes indexes.
   1. Love—Quotations, maxims, etc. I. Hobe,
Phyllis.
PN6084.L6W64 1982   082   82-8376
ISBN 0-664-26001-2   AACR2

Contents

Acknowledgments

"The Doctor's Prescription," by Charles L. Allen. From *The Charles L. Allen Treasury* by Charles L. Allen, copyright © 1970 by Fleming H. Revell Company. Used by permission.

"Be Loving," from *Because I Love You,* by Alice Joyce Davidson. Copyright © 1982 by Alice Joyce Davidson. Published by Fleming H. Revell Company. Used by permission.

"Long Lost Friends" and "Hold Fast" © 1959, 1967 by Marjorie Holmes Mighell. From the book *Love and Laughter,* by Marjorie Holmes. Reprinted by permission of Doubleday & Company, Inc.

"No East or West," by John Oxenham, is reprinted by permission of Desmond Dunkerley.

The poems of Helen Steiner Rice are reprinted by permission of Gibson Greeting Cards, Inc., Cincinnati, Ohio 45237.

Two excerpts from *In the Vineyard of the Lord,* by Helen Steiner Rice, copyright © 1979 by Helen Steiner Rice and Fred Bauer. Published by Fleming H. Revell Company. Used by permission.

"I Rose to Brother All," by Perry Tanksley, from *Love*

Introduction
by Marjorie Holmes

God is love.

To me this explains the whole wonder of love. For life itself begins with love. The wonder of love between man and woman . . . of mating and creation. . . . Then the newborn cradled in its mother's arms, drawing its first food from her warm breast, literally drinking in love. . . . The parents, the child, the family, bound in the circle of love. Yet a circle that stretches to embrace others—friends, relatives, neighbors, sweethearts. Until the circle breaks and re-forms into new families, new circles of love.

And in the process the sweetest, most noble and thrilling emotions are aroused. There is no wonder more sublime than to be in love. And nothing more rewarding, more fulfilling than to share a constantly growing love . . . with a husband or wife, a son or daughter, or a very dear friend. Only when we love and are loved are we truly happy. This is God's plan for us, his children. Without love, the problems and pains of life would be intolerable. To compensate, he has given us the wonder of love.

This little book celebrates that wonder in its many

guises. Through poetry, song, essay, and humor we are reminded of that vital and priceless gift from the Creator himself—love, human love.

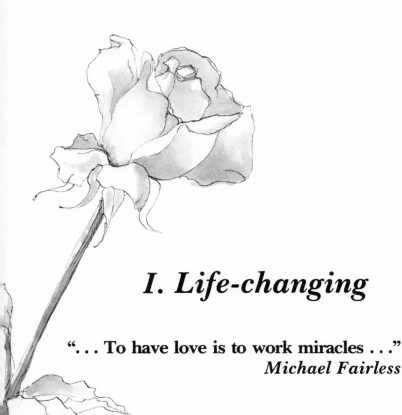

I. Life-changing

"... To have love is to work miracles ..."
Michael Fairless

WHAT IS LOVE?

What is love?
No words can define it,
It's something so great
Only God could design it. . . .
    Wonder of Wonders,
    Beyond man's conception,
    And only in God
    Can love find true perfection,
    For love means much more
    Than small words can express,
    For what man calls love
    Is so very much less
        Than the beauty and depth
        And the true richness of
        God's gift to mankind—
        His compassionate love. . . .
For love has become
A word that's misused,
Perverted, distorted
And often abused,
To speak of "light romance"
Or some affinity for
A passing attraction

That is seldom much more
Than a mere interlude
Of inflamed fascination,
A romantic fling
Of no lasting duration. . . .
      But love is enduring
      And patient and kind,
      It judges all things
      With the heart, not the mind,
      And love can transform
      The most commonplace
         Into beauty and splendor
         And sweetness and grace. . . .
For love is unselfish,
Giving more than it takes,
And no matter what happens
Love never forsakes,
It's faithful and trusting
And always believing,
Guileless and honest
And never deceiving. . . .
      Yes, love is beyond
      What man can define,
      For love is immortal
      And God's Gift is Divine!

Helen Steiner Rice

Whatever of love has touched a man's life has been touched by God.

Eugenia Price

HOW CAN I LOVE YOU?

There are times when I become so angry with a person that I want to say, "Get lost! You've had it!" That's the natural part of me—the limit of my human love. Then I remember how many times I've done some idiotic thing, the times I've hurt people, or the way I've misused the creation. Yet, God still loves me. He hasn't crossed me off his list, so how can I cross anybody off *my* list? Can't I see that when a person hurts me, he does it out of his need, his insecurity, or his pain? What good will it do for me to react to his behavior? He needs my love, not my vengeance. He needs some firm ground to stand on, some resources to fill his empty bucket. Something outside of me says, "There's another way to live—keep going back in love."

It isn't easy, it isn't natural to me, and I certainly can't claim the accomplishment for my own, but many times I am able to react in love when ordinarily I would reject in anger. The important thing is that my affirmation makes a difference not only in the life of the person who has hurt me but in my own life as well.

Louis H. Evans, Jr.

14

THE CALL OF LOVE

Let us never forget that the love of God has moral depth and it makes great demands. We sing silly little songs with titles such as "Somebody Up There Likes Me," and we talk about "The Man Upstairs," and we think of God's love as something that fits into a juke box. But God's love demands high living. When Jesus saw men of great promise giving themselves to fish nets, He said unto them, "Follow me, and I will make you fishers of men" (Matthew 4:19). Love calls to the highest life.

Charles L. Allen

He who finds not love finds nothing.

Spanish proverb

Talk not of wasted affection, affection never was wasted;
If it enrich not the heart of another, its waters, return-
    ing
Back to their springs, like the rain, shall fill them full of
    refreshment;
That which the fountain sends forth returns again to the
    fountain.

Henry Wadsworth Longfellow

15

This is the miracle that happens every time to those who really love: the more they give, the more they possess of that precious nourishing love from which flowers and children have their strength and which could help all human beings if they would take it without doubting.

Rainer Maria Rilke

The essence of all beauty, I call love.

Elizabeth Barrett Browning

To have faith is to create;
To have hope is to call down blessing;
To have love is to work miracles.

Michael Fairless

THE GLORY OF UNSELFISH LOVE

Now that I am seventy years old, and life is rapidly passing for me, if I should be asked how my discovery of the unselfishness of God affects my feelings towards old age and death, I could but say, that, secure in the knowledge that God is and that He is enough, I find old age delightful in the present, and death a prospect for the future.

If it were not for Him, old age with its failing powers and its many infirmities could not but be a sad and wearisome time; but, with God, our lovely unselfish God, at the back of it, old age is simply a delightful resting-place.

I have tried in my day to help bear the burdens of my own generation, and, now that that generation has almost passed away, I am more than happy to know that the responsibilities of the present generation do not rest upon me.

I admire the divine order that evidently lays upon each generation its own work, to be done in its own way; and I am convinced that, whether it may seem to us for good or for ill, the generation that is passing must give place to the one that is coming and must keep hands off from interfering.

Everything is safe when an unselfish love is guiding and controlling, and therefore my old heart is at rest, and I can lay down my arms with a happy confidence that, since God is in His heaven, all must necessarily be right with His world. And I can peacefully wait to understand what seems mysterious now, until the glorious day of revelation to which every hour brings me nearer.

Therefore with an easy mind I can look forward to death, and the prospect of leaving this life and of entering into the larger and grander life beyond is pure bliss to me. It is like having a new country, full of unknown marvels, to explore; and the knowledge that no one and nothing can hinder my going there is a secret spring of joy at the bottom of my heart.

I am like the butterfly just preparing to slip out of its old cocoon; panting for the life outside, but with no experience to tell it what kind of life that outside life will be. But I believe with all my heart that the apostle told the truth when he declared that, "Eye hath not seen, nor ear heard, neither hath it entered into the heart of man the things which God hath prepared for them that love him" (I Corinthians 2:9). And what better prospect could the soul have!

Then will be fulfilled the prayer of our Lord, "Father, I will that they also, whom thou hast given me, be with me where I am; that they may behold my glory which thou hast given me" (John 17:24).

That glory is not the glory of dazzling light but it is the glory of unselfish love. I have had a few faint glimpses of this glory now and here, and it has been enough to ravish my heart. But there I shall see Him as He is, in all the glory of an infinite unselfishness which no heart of man has even been able to conceive; and I await the moment with joy.

Hannah Whitall Smith

18

Being conscious of Christ's attention not only affected what I did and said, but what I *saw*. And just seeing people differently changed entire relationships. There was one man, whom I disliked intensely, whose office was close to ours. He was arrogant and a smart aleck; he needled people viciously, many of whom, like the secretaries, could only choke back tears of embarrassment and anger. This man was mad at the world. As an angry smart aleck (which is what I saw when I looked at him), he had no use for Christ's love. But as I began to look at this man, being aware that Christ and I were looking at him together, I began to see—in the same person—a man who was deeply hurt, threatened, and *very* lonely. This is what this man really was inside. It dawned on me that for a man like *that,* Christ's love could have meaning. When I responded naturally to what I now saw as I looked at this man, he began to drop the facade of anger, and the hurt began to come out. Suddenly we were at ease with each other *without anything having been said* to break down the wall. Just by trying to look from Christ's perspective, I saw the real person behind his mask, and somehow he knew and felt loved. I was seeing why the saints had come up with such seemingly simple, basic ways to relate. It was not because they were brilliant. Most of them were not. They had a different perspective; and from that spiritual vantage point, they looked at the unsolvable problems other men saw. However, they saw—in the same situations—different problems. They saw problems which *could* be dealt with through love and acceptance of God. They saw men as Christ saw them.

Keith Miller

Of all the music that reaches farthest into heaven, it is the beating of a loving heart.

Henry Ward Beecher

We like someone *because*. We love someone *although*.

Henri de Montherlant

Stand at the seashore, and watch the tide go out and the tide come in. There is no power on earth great enough to stop the tide, and that principle operates all through life: what goes out, comes in. Send out love, and love comes back. Send out hate, and hate comes back. Send out mercy, mercy comes back. What we give, we get.

Charles L. Allen

THE DOCTOR'S PRESCRIPTION

A doctor is prescribing for a group of sick people. After examination, he discovers they are filled with poisons that will not only eventually destroy their bodies, but rob them of all the joy and peace of life and eventually destroy their souls. He discovers they are filled with the poisons of envy, jealousy, selfishness and hate. Each one is thinking of himself as more important than any of his fellows. One says he is the finest public speaker. Another claims to be able to look into the future, while another feels he is better educated. Still another claims to do more for other people.

The wise doctor tells them no matter what abilities they may possess or what services they may render, if their hearts are not filled with love, they do not amount to anything. Then he analyzes his prescription of love. The doctor is St. Paul and you can read all this in I Corinthians 13.

Love is not a single thing, but a composite of many things.

1. Love "suffereth long." This is the attitude of love. To be patient means to possess endurance under stress or annoyance. Love works today while it waits for tomorrow.

On the desk of a very fine businessman I saw the motto, "This, too, shall pass." He told me that that motto had saved him many times. No matter how bad the storm may be, if you are sure that one day it will blow out and the sun will shine again, you will never give up.

2. "And is kind." That is the activity of love. . . . A man once said about his sick wife, "There is nothing I

would not do for her." One of the neighbors replied, "That is just the trouble. You have been doing nothing for her for forty years."

3. Love "envieth not." As Henry Drummond, who wrote the greatest sermon in existence on this chapter, said, "This is love in competition with others." Envy leads to hate and hate destroys a soul. Love always congratulates.

4. Love is humble—"vaunteth not itself, is not puffed up." Love and conceit are contradictory terms. What God wants is men great enough to be small enough to be used. Love takes a towel, girds itself, and gets on its knees to do a menial task that lesser men are too big to do.

5. "Doth not behave itself unseemly." Love is courteous. Love possesses tact and good manners. The old, old saying is still true: "Politeness is to do and say, the kindest thing in the kindest way." Love never wants to offend, it never demands its rights, it is respectful and is ever mindful of the desires and comforts of others.

6. "Seeketh not her own." The greatest verse in the Bible tells us: "For God so loved the world that he gave . . ." (John 3:16). Love is always more concerned with what it can give than with what it can get. Love is seeking to minister unto. Love understands that it is, "Not what we gain but what we give, that measures the worth of the life we live."

7. "Is not easily provoked." Love is good-tempered. This is a lack that many people brag about. They tell you about their temper as if it were a great asset. But it is no credit to be able to get mad.

There are two types of sins—the sins of the body and the sins of the disposition; both are bad but of the two, I would rather be in the company of some prodigal who went to the far country than some elder brother who stayed at home and lived a moral life yet had a bad disposition. Love knows how to keep certain emotions cool.

8. "Thinketh no evil; rejoiceth not in iniquity." Love is not suspicious and never accuses merely on rumor. Love believes the best of every person until proven wrong. And if some person does go wrong, love is not secretly glad and does not gossip about it.

9. "Beareth all things." Love bears its burdens with dignity, continues to believe, never loses hope and endures to the end.

Charles L. Allen

We miss the spirit of Christmas if we consider the incarnation as an indistinct and doubtful, far-off event unrelated to our present problems. We miss the purport of Christ's birth if we do not accept it as a living link which joins us together in spirit as children of the everliving and true God. In love alone—the love of God and the love of man—will be found the solution of all the ills which afflict the world today. Slowly, sometimes painfully, but always with increasing purpose, emerges the great message of Christianity: Only with wisdom comes joy, and with greatness comes love.

Harry S Truman

23

II. Goodness

"... a humble, low-born thing ..."
James Russell Lowell

Not what we give, but what we share,—
For the gift without the giver is bare;
Who gives himself with his alms feeds three,—
Himself, his hungering neighbor, and me.

James Russell Lowell

Kindness is a language which
the blind can see and the deaf can
hear.

Anonymous

Kind words toward those you daily meet,
    Kind words and actions right,
Will make this life of ours most sweet,
    Turn darkness into light.

Isaac Watts

TRUE LOVE

True love is but a humble, low-born thing,
And hath its food served up in earthenware;
It is a thing to walk with, hand in hand,
Through the everydayness of this work-day world,
Baring its tender feet to every roughness,
Yet letting not one heart-beat go astray
From beauty's law of plainness and content—
A simple, fireside thing, whose quiet smile
Can warm earth's poorest hovel to a home.

James Russell Lowell

most of my real friends are not church leaders. not
ministers or board members or administrators of the
church. they live on ordinary streets, behind plain
doors, with down-to-earth hearts. they are realistic
about human nature. they have lived and they have
failed and they are honest about being fragile. they can
somehow grasp the enormous love of Christ. their
hearts are fertile soil for God to live in. they know that
without love, we are nothing . . . and love is

> compassion, meekness, longsuffering,
> gentleness, patience, forgiveness.

their response to life teaches me that God is LOVE.

Ann Kiemel

WHEN LOVE
IS KIND

When Love is kind,
Cheerful and free,
Love's sure to find
Welcome from me!

But when Love brings
Heartache or pang,
Tears and such things—
Love may go bang!

If Love can sigh
For one alone,
Well pleased am I
To be that one.

But should I see
Love giv'n to rove
To two or three,
Then—good-bye, Love!

Love must, in short,
Keep fond and true,
Through good report,
And evil too.

Else, here I swear,
Young Love may go,
For aught I care—
To Jericho.

Thomas Moore

JUST A WORD

It's no trick at all
When you've had a fall
To patch up the skin you have broken;
But it's something again
To heal up the pain,
The hurt, of an ugly word spoken.

You can't call it back
Nor heal up the crack
That's made in the heart of a dear one;
A double-edged sword
Is each ugly word—
As harmful to say as to hear one.

Anonymous

To love anyone is nothing else
than to wish that person good.

Thomas Aquinas

DAY TO DAY

The more you love, the more you'll find
That life is good and friends are kind . . .
    For only What We Give Away
    Enriches Us from Day to Day.

Helen Steiner Rice

LIVING BY GRACE

Grace is doing for another being kindnesses he doesn't deserve, hasn't earned, could not ask for, and can't repay. Its main facets are beauty, kindness, gratitude, charm, favor, and thankfulness. Grace offers man what he cannot do for himself. The unwritten creed of many is that God is under obligation to them, but grace suggests that we are under obligation to God. To live in that consciousness is to live by grace. Living by grace is costly; it means sharing. It has no meaning apart from a spirit of self-sacrifice that prompts the soul to think more of giving than of receiving, of caring for others rather than for one's self.

Paul McElroy

III. Friendship

". . . Walk beside me . . ."
Albert Camus

IN GRATITUDE FOR FRIENDS

I thank You, God in Heaven, for friends.
When morning wakes, when daytime ends,
   I have the consciousness
Of loving hands that touch my own,
Of tender glance and gentle tone,
   Of thoughts that cheer and bless!
If sorrow comes to me I know
That friends will walk the way I go,
   And, as the shadows fall,
I know that I will raise my eyes
And see—ah, hope that never dies!—
   The dearest Friend of All.

Margaret E. Sangster

A friend is a present you give
yourself.

Robert Louis Stevenson

A friend may well be reckoned
the masterpiece of nature.

Ralph Waldo Emerson

It is my joy in life to find
   At every turning of the road
The strong arms of a comrade kind
   To help me onward with my load.
And since I have no gold to give
   And love alone can make amends,
My only prayer is, "While I live,
   God, make me worthy of my friends!"

Author unknown

A friend is one
to whom one may pour
out all the contents
of one's heart,
chaff and grain together,
knowing that the
gentlest of hands
will take and sift it,
keep what is worth keeping
and with a breath of kindness
blow the rest away.

Arabian proverb

One of the most beautiful qualities of true friendship is to understand and to be understood.

Seneca

Instead of a gem or a flower, cast the gift of a lovely thought into the heart of a friend.

George Macdonald

LONG LOST FRIENDS

It happens in almost every house:

The phone rings and you hear the voice of some friend, relative (or friend of a friend or relative) so long lost you grope to place the identity. "Why—why, how wonderful," you exclaim. "Where are you?"

And as they admit they are either in the city or approaching it, "Gracious, we'd just love to see you—" even as you make frantic calculations: How many beds can we make up? Did those towels get back from the laundry? "You—you must come out for dinner." And as they demur that they wouldn't want to put you to any trouble, you not only insist, you find yourself urging that they spend the night. No, no, it won't put you out a bit, you won't do a *thing*.

Hanging up, you gaze wildly about the tumbled house. And food! You can hardly feed them the intended leftovers and it's too late to thaw a roast; you'll have to go to the store. Meanwhile, you start barking orders: "Pat, go clean up your room, they'll have to sleep there—you can have the couch. Freddy, put those puzzles away and sweep the rug. Janey, go out in the yard with Jimmy and see if you can find enough dry branches to start a fire. Also, anything that remotely resembles flowers. Now *hurry*, everybody, they should be here in an hour."

And you go galloping off to the grocery intent only on steak for supper, bacon for breakfast, lettuce, some rolls—and spend twenty dollars. And there's a long line before the cashier, it takes longer than you thought; and as you finally come panting into the homestretch, you see, with sinking heart, the out-of-state car.

They've found a shortcut, they announce triumphantly over the kisses and exclamations—here they are!

And the fireplace that should be blazing brightly is stone cold. Janey comes in with three frostbitten, bedraggled weeds. The sweeper's dead center of the rug while Freddy gazes transfixed at the TV set. And why, oh why didn't you at least put on a skirt before going to the store?

But, still frowsy and frenzied, you strive to be the cordial hostess even as you stash some groceries away, snatch out others. And if your husband is going to have

35

all these relatives why can't he get home and help entertain them? And thank goodness here he is to make the fire and mix the drinks and bolster conversation while you get dinner on.

And between courses you slip to the basement to check the sheets and signal a daughter to iron them before the evening's over, hoping she doesn't get the one with the mended place in the middle. And where did you put those thick bright Christmas-present towels?

And you sit up late visiting, showing home movies, getting acquainted or reacquainted, and there is a sense of fellowship, of warmth and goodness and drawing together that compensates for the confusion. And when at last you are all bedded down you whisper to your husband, "They're really lovely, aren't they? I'm really glad they came."

And in the morning you linger over a fresh pot of coffee after the children are off to school. You find yourselves urging, "You don't have to go on today, do you? Can't we show you around?" And when the hearty thanks and farewells have been said, you wave at the departing car with a curious sense of loss. "Good-by, good-by, come back soon!" you call—and mean it.

It's been worth all the trouble.

Marjorie Holmes

Greater love hath no man than this,
that a man lay down his life for his friends.

John 15:13

When, in disgrace with fortune and men's eyes,
I all alone beweep my outcast state
And trouble deaf heaven with my bootless cries
And look upon myself and curse my fate,
Wishing me like to one more rich in hope,
Featured like him, like him with friends possessed,
Desiring this man's art and that man's scope,
With what I most enjoy contented least;
Yet in these thoughts myself almost despising,
Haply I think on thee, and then my state,
Like to the lark at break of day arising
From sullen earth, sings hymns at heaven's gate;
   For thy sweet love remembered such wealth brings
   That then I scorn to change my state with kings.

William Shakespeare

Blest be the tie that binds
Our hearts in Christian love;
The fellowship of kindred minds
Is like to that above.

Before our Father's throne
We pour our ardent prayers;
Our fears, our hopes, our aims are one,
Our comforts and our cares.

We share each other's woes,
Each other's burdens bear;
And often for each other flows
The sympathizing tear.

When for a while we part,
This thought will soothe our pain,
That we shall still be joined in heart
And one day meet again.

One glorious hope revives
Our courage by the way;
While each in expectation lives
And longs to see the day,

When from all toil and pain
And sin we shall be free,
And perfect love and friendship reign
Through all eternity.

John Fawcett

The glory of friendship is not the outstretched hand, nor the kindly smile nor the joy of companionship; it is the spirited inspiration that comes to one when he discovers that someone else believes in him and is willing to trust him.

Ralph Waldo Emerson

Don't walk in front of me
   I may not follow
Don't walk behind me
   I may not lead
Walk beside me
And just be my friend.

Albert Camus

I looked for my soul
but my soul I could not see.
I looked for my God
but my God eluded me.
I looked for a friend
and then I found all three.

Anonymous

The more we love, the better we are;
and the greater our friendships are,
the dearer we are to God.

Jeremy Taylor

The older I grow in years, the more the wonder and the joy increase when I see the power of these words of Jesus—"I have called you friends"—to move the human heart. To the rich and poor alike, to the learned and ignorant, they bring with them a message of peace and love. They are "spirit" and "life"; and the results that follow are manifest.

The awe that rises in our hearts when the knowledge dawns at last that he has said to us, "You are my friends," passes on into confidence and joy. That one word "friend" breaks down each barrier of reserve, and we have boldness in his presence. Our hearts go out in love to meet his love.

C. F. Andrews

The only rose without thorns is friendship.

Madeline DeScudery

40

CONFIDE IN A FRIEND

When you're tired and worn at the close of day
And things just don't seem to be going your way,
When even your patience has come to an end,
Try taking time out and confide in a friend.

Author unknown

Until I truly loved, I was alone.

Caroline Norton

There is no heaven like mutual
love.

George Granville

LOVE IS NOT BLIND

Love is *not* blind. Love has 20/20 spiritual vision.

The eyes of love are open, clear, penetrating, serene. . . .

Loves sees through all colors of skin to the child of God.

Love sees deep into the human heart to discover the goodness there.

Love sees through intolerance, prejudice, misunderstanding to brotherhood.

Love sees through conflict, struggle and separation to the unity of all life.

Love sees through the darkness of discouragement and despair to the shining light of hope.

Love sees the blossom in the rosebud, the greatness in the common man.

Love sees the criminal, the drug addict, the alcoholic, the forsaken and abandoned transformed by the miracle of the spirit within.

Love sees men at war not as enemies to kill, but as friends gone astray who must be won back to sanity and good will.

Love sees the silver lining in the storm clouds.

Love sees through defeat to victory, through disease to healing, through problems to solutions, through hate to forgiveness, through unhappiness to joy, through fear to courage, through unbelief to faith, through evil to good.

Love sees heaven on earth.

Love is *not* blind. The most powerful sight in the world is the insight of love.

Love sees with the eyes of God, for God is love.

Wilfred A. Peterson

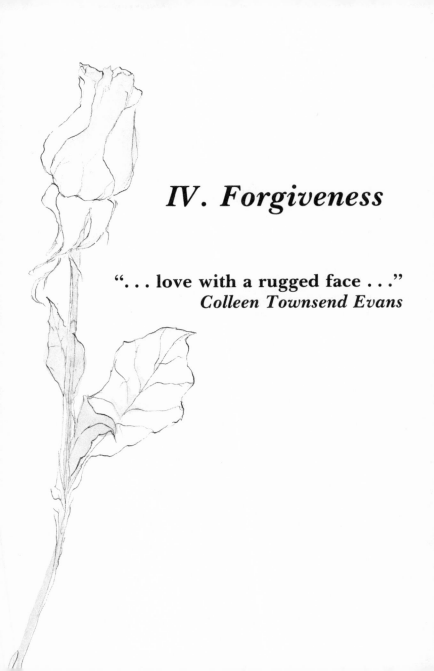

IV. Forgiveness

"... love with a rugged face ..."
Colleen Townsend Evans

"BUT I LIKE YOU"

The game of Cowboys and Indians had been going on vigorously and, to stretch the meaning of the word a little, peacefully, out on the beach for some time. Then, suddenly, there was trouble.

One of the youngsters, a brown-haired Cowboy, about seven and the youngest of the lot, had been captured by the Indians and was to be tied to a stake—the stake being a huge, ugly hunk of driftwood that looked very much like the gnarled roots of an ancient tree. The brown-haired Cowboy objected to being tied to the driftwood. Whether, in his concept of the game, the driftwood was not legitimately a stake or whether he, out of some special sensitivity, found the ugly driftwood objectionable, I could not make out. But he was very definite about it. He would not be tied to it.

The boss of the game, the oldest of the boys, about ten or eleven and something of a bully, grew angry.

"Go on home, Yellow!" he shouted at the little fellow. "Go on home. We don't like you!"

The other boys, in the natural spirit of the gang, took up the words in a sort of singsong. "Go on home, Yellow! We don't like you!"

The boy, hurt and bewildered by this sudden show of

cruelty, looked from one face to another. Then, after a long moment, in a voice quavering but deeply earnest, he said, "But I like you."

The singsong stopped before his earnestness. For a brief moment, it seemed as if his simple but gravely moving words would have some effect. Three of the boys looked at one another in uncertainty. They had been somehow touched.

But the bully had not been touched. "Go on home, Yellow!" he cried out again. And then to the gang, "Come on, fellers! Let's go!"

The game was begun again without the brown-haired Cowboy.

He looked desolately on for a minute or two, then turned and moved slowly away, following the frothing white line of the sea's edge, sadness in his drooping figure, bewilderment still on his sensitive face.

I watched him go. I felt profoundly sorry for him. It was as if I had just watched the stoning of a prophet.

He grew smaller in the distance. Still his words stayed with me.

"But I like you."

It is a long way from a mountain in Galilee to the beach at Malibu and today's world, yet that brown-haired boy, standing there on the sand, answering his young tormentors with an earnest declaration of his affection for them, vividly brought back to me those dramatic, revolutionary words, "But I say unto you, love your enemies . . ."

He disappeared from my view around a wide sweep of the shore.

Myles Connolly

If I hate or despise any one man in the world, I hate something that God cannot hate, and despise that which he loves. And though many people may appear to us ever so sinful, odious, or extravagant in their conduct, we must never look upon that, as the least motive for any contempt or disregard of them; but look upon them with the greater compassion, as being in the most pitiable condition that can be.

William Law

I consider myself as the most wretched of men, full of sores and corruption, and who has committed all sorts of crimes against his King. Touched with a sensible regret, I confess to Him all my wickedness, I ask His forgiveness, I abandon myself in His hands that He may do what He pleases with me. The King, full of mercy and goodness, very far from chastising me, embraces me with love, makes me eat at His table, serves me with His own hands, gives me the key of His treasures; He converses and delights Himself with me incessantly, in a thousand and a thousand ways, and treats me in all respects as His favorite. It is thus I consider myself from time to time in His holy presence.

Brother Lawrence

A little girl once ... asked whether the Lord Jesus always forgave us for our sins as soon as we asked Him, and I had said, "Yes, of course He does." "*Just* as soon?" she repeated doubtingly. "Yes," I replied, "the very minute we ask, He forgives us." "Well," she said deliberately, "I cannot believe that. I should think He would make us feel sorry for two or three days first. And then I should think He would make us ask Him a great many times, and in a very pretty way too, not just in common talk. And I believe that *is* the way He does, and you need not try to make me think He forgives me right at once, no matter what the Bible says." She only *said* what most Christians *think,* and what is worse, what most Christians act on, making their discouragement and their very remorse separate them infinitely further off from God than their sin would have done. Yet it is so totally contrary to the way we like our children to act toward us, that I wonder how we ever could have conceived such an idea of God. How a mother grieves when a naughty child goes off alone in despairing remorse, and doubts her willingness to forgive; and how ... her whole heart goes out in welcoming love to the repentant little one who ... begs her forgiveness! Surely our God felt this yearning love when He said to us, "Return, ye backsliding children, and I will heal your backslidings."

The fact is, that the same moment which brings the consciousness of sin ought to bring also the confession and the consciousness of forgiveness. This is especially essential to an unwavering walk in the "life hid with Christ in God," for no separation from Him can be tolerated here for an instant.

Hannah Whitall Smith

And so throughout eternity
I forgive you, you forgive me;
As our dear Redeemer said,
This is the Wine, this is the Bread.

William Blake

While there is no sin God cannot forgive, his love is not a holy cover-up. Nor is he a pushover. When we feel God's forgiving mercy in our lives, we are not to withhold that same mercy from others. . . . But that doesn't mean we are to wink at evil. Forgiveness does not allow a fool to persist in folly . . . or lies to go unchallenged . . . or prejudice to flourish unopposed. Forgiveness is reality dealing sensibly with reality—love with a rugged face.

Colleen Townsend Evans

When Leonardo da Vinci was working on his painting "The Last Supper," he became angry with a certain man. Losing his temper he lashed the other fellow with bitter words and threats. Returning to his canvas he attempted to work on the face of Jesus, but was unable to do so. He was so upset he could not compose himself for the painstaking work. Finally he put down his tools and sought out the man and asked his forgiveness. The man accepted his apology and Leonardo was able to return to his workshop and finish painting the face of Jesus.

Author unknown

In a novel that was popular a few years ago, one of the characters made a statement that became quite famous: "Love means you never have to say you're sorry." Well, I'm afraid I have to disagree. For me, love means you *do* say you're sorry. . . . You don't hit the bottle, pull the trigger, become unbearable with those close to you, or bore people with your cynicism. You face what you have done and you repent . . . and then you allow God to love you back to health.

Colleen Townsend Evans

I don't like to think of myself as someone who could deliberately do wrong . . . and yet I know there is that potential in me because I am human. Like the Quaker who saw a man going to the gallows and said, "There, but for the grace of God, go I," you and I cannot claim credit for the times we do not sin. The occasions are many and the temptations are powerful—much too powerful for us to resist. We need help. . . . As much as we tell ourselves that we could never do such things as we condemn in others, the truth is, we *can*. And we do. Whether our sins are large or small, monstrous or "human," seen or unseen, we commit them. It is our human condition—and on our own we aren't strong enough to do otherwise.

But Someone Else is. . . . Someone Else can help us put another person's need before our own. . . . Someone Else can open our eyes to the fact that "everybody" may be wrong. Someone Else knows that, in spite of the headlines of our lives, we are not what we sometimes seem to be. Someone Else knows that there is a potential for goodness in each of us. He put it there—and with his help we can reach it.

Colleen Townsend Evans

God already knows all about us. Confession is our recognition that what we have done is wrong; it also means our desire to have it taken out of our lives and hearts. We do not need to persuade God to forgive. As we look at the cross we realize that He loves us and goes to the uttermost for us.

Charles L. Allen

V. Family

"... To hold each other fast ..."
Marjorie Holmes

A house is built of logs and stone,
  Of tiles and posts and piers;
A home is built of loving deeds
  That stand a thousand years.

Victor Hugo

Love is the joyous conflict of two or more free self-conscious persons who rejoice in one another's individualities and through the clash of mind on mind and will on will work out an ever-increasing but never finally completed unity. And the primary school of this vital and vitalizing love is the home.

G. A. Studdert-Kennedy

A man is not where he lives, but where he loves.

Latin proverb

MY HEART'S IN THE HIGHLANDS

My heart's in the Highlands, my heart is not here;
My heart's in the Highlands a-chasing the deer;
A-chasing the wild deer, and following the roe,—
My heart's in the Highlands wherever I go.

Farewell to the Highlands, farewell to the North,
The birthplace of valor, the country of worth;
Wherever I wander, wherever I rove,
The hills of the Highlands for ever I love.

Farewell to the mountains high covered with snow;
Farewell to the straths and green valleys below;
Farewell to the forests and wild-hanging woods;
Farewell to the torrents and loud-pouring floods.

My heart's in the Highlands, my heart is not here;
My heart's in the Highlands a-chasing the deer,
A-chasing the wild deer, and following the roe,—
My heart's in the Highlands wherever I go.

Robert Burns

TO HUSBAND AND WIFE

Preserve sacredly the privacies of your own house, your married state and your heart. Let no one ever presume to come between you or share the joys or sorrows that belong to you two alone.

With mutual help, build your quiet world, not allowing your dearest earthly friend to be the confidant of aught that concerns your domestic peace. Let moments of alienation, if they occur, be healed at once. Never, never speak of it outside; but to each other confess, and all will come out right. Never let the morrow's sun still find you at variance. Renew and renew your vow. It will do you good; and thereby your minds will grow together contented in the love which is stronger than death, and you will be truly one.

Author unknown

BELIEVE ME, IF ALL THOSE ENDEARING YOUNG CHARMS

Believe me, if all those endearing young charms,
Which I gaze on so fondly to-day,
Were to change by to-morrow, and fleet in my arms,
Like fairy-gifts fading away,
Thou wouldst still be adored, as this moment thou art,
Let thy loveliness fade as it will,
And around the dear ruin each wish of my heart
Would entwine itself verdantly still.

Thomas Moore

TO MY WIFE

Trusty, dusky, vivid, true,
With eyes of gold and bramble-dew,
Steel true and blade straight
The Great Artificer made my mate.

Honor, anger, valor, fire,
A love that life could never tire,
Death quench nor evil stir,
The Mighty Master gave to her.

Teacher, tender comrade, wife,
A fellow-farer true through life,
Heart-whole and soul-free,
The August Father gave to me.

Robert Louis Stevenson

TO MY DEAR AND LOVING HUSBAND

If ever two were one, then surely we.
If ever man were lov'd by wife, then thee.
If ever wife was happy in a man,
Compare with me, ye women, if you can.
I prize thy love more than whole Mines of gold,
Or all the riches that the East doth hold.
My love is such that Rivers cannot quench,
Nor ought but love from thee give recompence.
Thy love is such I can no way repay;
The heavens reward thee manifold I pray.
Then while we live, in love let's so persever,
That when we live no more, we may live ever.

Anne Bradstreet

Ofttimes across the room you come
To press a kiss against my hair,
To hold me for no cause at all,
Save love. At once our small ones there
Come laughing, making a ring-around.
So does devotion strike a spark
That showers into golden light,
Gathering children in its arc.

Virginia Moody Hagan

HOLD FAST

Watch it with wonder, hold it fast—the gangling length of a little boy, the slender, tender dimensions of a fast-growing little girl . . .

You test this state of growing more often than not just after a meal. For you are sitting at the table, and they are just leaving their chairs. It seems you must reach out to them an instant before they go. "Come sit on my lap a minute, let's see how big you are."

And quickly, if sometimes a bit shyly, they oblige. Grinning, they settle themselves upon your inadequate knees. Cocking their heads to show they are really a bit beyond all this, yet with the relaxed enjoyment of animals still taking comfort in the nest, they cuddle, arms about your neck.

"Can't do this much longer, Mother, soon we'll be bigger than you."

"Okay, it'll be my turn then, you'll have to hold me."

They not only fervently promise, the prospect so intrigues them they sometimes insist on clambering down and trying you on their spindly laps for size . . .

To draw near to one another, that is the main thing. To hold each other fast. Physical demonstrations of affection are as needful in the human family as food. To restrain them may be to walk the cold and proper road to adult dignity, but it is also to stunt the emotions and starve the heart.

Hold your children in your arms as long as you can. And when you can't, let them hold you!

Marjorie Holmes

I AM THE CHILD

I am the child.
All the world waits for my coming.
And the earth watches with interest
To see what I shall become.
Civilization hangs in the balance,
For what I am
The world of tomorrow will be.

I am the child.
I have come into your world,
About which I knew nothing.
Why I come I know not.
How I came I know not.
I am curious; I am interested.

I am the child.
You hold in your hand my destiny.
You determine, largely,
Whether I shall succeed or fail.
Give me, I pray you, those things
That make for happiness.
Train me, I beg you, that I may be
A blessing to the world.

Mamie Gene Cole

WHAT SORT OF A FATHER ARE YOU?

What sort of a father are you to your boy?
  Do you know if your standing is good?
Do you ever take stock of yourself and check up
  Your accounts with your boy as you should?

Do you ever reflect on your conduct with him?
  Are you all that a father should be?
Do you send him away when you're anxious to read
  Or let him climb up on your knee?

Have you time to bestow on the boy when he comes
  With his questions—to tell him the truth?
Or do you neglect him, and leave him alone
  To work out the problems of youth?

Do you ever go walking with him, hand in hand?
  Do you plan little outings for him?
Does he ever look forward to camping with you?
  Or are you eternally grim?

Come, father, reflect! Does he know you today?
  And do you know him as you should?
Is gold so important to you that you leave
  It to chance that your boy will be good?

Take stock of yourself and consider the lad,
  Your time and your thoughts are his due.
How would you answer your God should He ask
  What sort of a father are you?

Author unknown

A LITTLE FELLOW
FOLLOWS ME

A careful man I ought to be,
A little fellow follows me,
I do not dare to go astray
For fear he'll go the selfsame way.

Not once can I escape his eyes;
Whate'er he sees me do he tries.
Like me, says he's going to be
That little chap who follows me.

He thinks that I am good and fine;
Believes in every word of mine.
The base in me he must not see
That little chap who follows me.

I must remember as I go,
Thro' summer sun and winter snow,
I'm building for the years to be
That little chap who follows me.

Author unknown

THE CHILDREN'S HOUR

Between the dark and the daylight,
  When the night is beginning to lower,
Comes a pause in the day's occupations,
  That is known as the Children's Hour.

I hear in the chamber above me
  The patter of little feet,
The sound of a door that is opened
  And voices soft and sweet.

From my study I see in the lamplight,
  Descending the broad hall stair,
Grave Alice, and laughing Allegra
  And Edith with golden hair.

A whisper, and then a silence:
  Yet I know by their merry eyes
They are plotting and planning together
  To take me by surprise.

A sudden rush from the stairway,
  A sudden raid from the hall!
By three doors left unguarded
  They enter my castle wall!

Do you think, O blue-eyed banditti,
  Because you have scaled the wall,
Such an old moustache as I am
  Is not a match for you all!

I have you fast in my fortress,
  And will not let you depart,
But put you down into the dungeon
  In the round-tower of my heart.

And there will I keep you forever,
  Yes, forever and a day,
Till the wall shall crumble to ruin,
  And moulder in dust away!

Henry Wadsworth Longfellow

OF A SMALL DAUGHTER
WALKING OUTDOORS

Easy, wind!
Go softly here!
She is small
And very dear.

She is young
And cannot say
Words to chase
The wind away.

She is new
To walking, so,
Wind, be kind
And gently blow

On her ruffled head,
On grass and clover.
Easy, wind . . .
She'll tumble over!

Frances M. Frost

GOD BLESS YOU, DEAR

God bless you, dear, for happiness;
For loving me;
For things of beauty in this life
You help me to see;

For sharing burdens that are mine;
For gentleness;
For tears you've dried, for words you've said
That live to bless;

For laughter, fun, the little things
Of every day;
For teaching me the way to turn
Work into play;

For qualities of mind and heart
Nobly expressed;
For courage, honor, kindness, faith
That meet each test;

For changing drab days into gold
And shining hours;
For facing storms as calmly as
The summer showers.

Your tender smile and warmth of love
Are always near;
For everything you are to me,
God bless you, dear.

Isla Paschal Richardson

VI. In Action

"... the greatest of these is love ..."
I Corinthians 13:13

Brothers, love the whole of God's creation, all of it down to the very dust. Love each leaf, each ray of God's light, love animals, love plants, love everything. If you love everything, you will understand the mystery of God in things. Once you see this, you will go on understanding it better every day. And eventually you will love the world with a love that includes every single thing. Love animals: God has given them a kind of thought and a tranquil enjoyment. Do not disturb it, do not hurt them, do not spoil their happiness, do not go contrary to God's purposes for them. Love little children especially, for they are innocent as angels; they are given to us as a sign, to touch and cleanse our hearts.

Fyodor Dostoevsky

Love communicates an immense
value to our smallest actions.

Auguste Saudreau

By love I do not mean any natural tenderness, which is more or less in people according to their constitution; but I mean a larger principle of the soul, founded in reason and piety, which makes us tender, kind and gentle to all our fellow creatures of God, and for his sake.

William Law

BE LOVING

To bring a bit of heaven
Down to earth from high above,
God blessed the world abundantly
With many kinds of love—
The love within a family,
The love of man and wife,
The love for creatures large and small,
And all that's good in life.
And every bit of love we show,
Each act of love we do,
Brings us closer yet to heaven
And to God who loves us, too!

Alice Joyce Davidson

Duty makes us do things well, but love makes us do them beautifully.

Phillips Brooks

LOVE ALWAYS LOOKS FOR A WAY OF BEING CONSTRUCTIVE

We learn and we grow much more by affirmation than by criticism. That doesn't mean that we can't encounter persons close to us. They need our honesty—provided they are convinced of our love—and I think they need that in larger proportions.

One day I was watching a young mother and her little boy in the backyard next door to a house where I was visiting, and I saw a beautiful demonstration of constructive loving. The mother was relaxing in a lounge chair, reading a book. The little boy was piling blocks, one on top of another, into wobbly totem poles that kept toppling to the ground. The child was becoming more frustrated with each failure; still, he kept on trying. Some parents, seeing those blocks tumbling down for the umpteenth time, would have screamed, "Put those things away!" But this young mother noted the child's frustration, put her book away, and sat down next to him, saying, "Come on, let's try it again." Giving the child a hug, she took some of the blocks and showed him how to pile them up more sturdily, until finally, between the two of them, they erected a formidable pillar. The child was completely delighted with his achievement and went on to play with something else.

Louis H. Evans, Jr.

Think lovingly, speak lovingly, act lovingly, and your every need shall be supplied; you shall not walk in desert places, . . . no danger shall overtake you.

James Allen

ALL INSIDE

Last eve I walked a certain street
  And met such gloomy folk;
I made great haste to pass them by,
  And neither smiled nor spoke.
The giant elms dropped sullenly,
  The very sun was dim—
I met a friend, and said, "I hope
  I've seen the last of him."

Today I walked the selfsame street,
  And loved the folks I met;
If business had not made me leave
  I would have been there yet.
Of course, I've solved the mystery,
  'Tis very plain to see;
The day I met the gloomy folks,
  The gloom was inside me!

Author unknown

All the beautiful sentiments in
the world weigh less than a single
lovely action.

James Russell Lowell

I am in love with this world. . . .
I have tilled its soil, I have gath-
ered its harvests, I have waited
upon its seasons, and always have I
reaped what I have sown.

John Burroughs

DIRT FARMER

He finds beauty among these simple things;
   The path a plow makes in the rich, red loam,
Gay sun-gold in ripe wheat—a plover's wings—
   A cow-bell, tinkling as the herd comes home.

He treads the soil, with earth-love in heart;
   Watches the young crops spring from fertile ground,
Loves the warm rain that makes the peach buds start,
   Land—and a man—in close communion bound!

Arden Antony

Appreciation is love returned. It
is man's best pay.

Lawrence Giles

I have found . . .
> that those who love a deer, a dog, a bird
>> and flowers . . .
> are usually thoughtful of the larger
>> needs that may be ours . . .
> . . . Who for God's creatures small will plan . . .
> will seldom wrong his fellow man.

Author unknown

LEARNING TO LOVE

There are many who want me to tell them of secret
ways of becoming perfect and I can only tell them that
the sole secret is a hearty love of God, and the only way
of attaining that love is by loving. You learn to speak by
speaking, to study by studying, to run by running, to
work by working; and just so you learn to love God and
man by loving. Begin as a mere apprentice and the very
power of love will lead you on to become a master of the
art.

St. Francis de Sales

Love vaunteth not itself, is not puffed up,
Doth not behave itself unseemly,
Seeketh not its own,
Is not easily provoked,
Thinketh no evil;
Rejoiceth not in iniquity, but rejoiceth in the truth;
Beareth all things,
Believeth all things,
Hopeth all things,
Endureth all things.
Love never faileth:
But whether there be prophecies, they shall fail;
Whether there be tongues, they shall cease;
Whether there be knowledge, it shall vanish away.
For we know in part, and we prophesy in part.
But when that which is perfect is come, then
That which is in part shall be done away.
When I was a child, I spake as a child,
I understood as a child, I thought as a child:
But when I became a man, I put away childish things.
For now we see through a glass, darkly;
But then face to face:
Now I know in part;
But then shall I know even as also I am known.
 And now abideth faith, hope, love, these three;
But the greatest of these is love.

I Corinthians 13:4–13

Don't dwell on your shortcomings. Focus all your attention on others, and you will find, in giving your love and attention to others, you, too, will be enriched.

Helen Steiner Rice

GETTING ENOUGH TO GIVE TO OTHERS

When I was growing up as a new Christian, I used to hear this explanation of joy: "Jesus first, others second, and yourself third." I suppose there is some truth to that, but *after* an important filling has taken place. We cannot give out of an empty bucket. We must receive before we have anything to give.

". . . love the Lord your God. . . . This is the great and first commandment. And a second is like it, You shall love your neighbor *as* yourself" (Matthew 22:37–39, italics added). That means "in the same manner as." As what? As you love yourself. In other words, if you don't know how to love yourself, how can you know how to love others? Remember the golden rule: "Do unto others as you would have them do to you." One has to have some idea of what would feel good before he can do good to another.

Louis H. Evans, Jr.

Christmas, my child, is love in action. . . . When you love someone, you *give* to them, as God gives to us. The greatest gift He ever gave was the Person of His Son, sent to us in human form so that we might know what God the Father is really like! Every time we love, every time we give, it's Christmas!

Dale Evans Rogers

Love seeks not limits but outlets.

Anonymous

There is no love which does not become help.

Paul Tillich

VII. Brotherhood

"... We drew a circle
that took him in ..."
Edwin Markham

Beloved, let us love one another:
for love is of God; and every one
that loveth is born of God, and
knoweth God.

I John 4:7

OUTWITTED

He drew a circle that shut me out—
Heretic, rebel, a thing to flout.
But Love and I had the wit to win:
We drew a circle that took him in!

Edwin Markham

And when with grief you see your brother stray
Or in a night of error lose his way,
Direct his wandering and restore the day . . .
Leave to avenging Heaven his stubborn will,
For, O, remember, he's your brother still.

Jonathan Swift

Ah, dear soul, if you have ever known this, even for a few hours, in any earthly relation; if you have ever loved any of your fellow human beings enough to find sacrifice and service on their behalf a joy; if a whole-souled abandonment of your will to the will of another has ever gleamed across you as a blessed and longed-for privilege, longing love of your Heavenly Lover would I entreat you to let it be so towards Christ!

He loves you with more than the love of friendship. As a bridegroom rejoices over his bride, so does He rejoice over you, and nothing but the bride's surrender will satisfy Him. He has given you all, and He asks for all in return. The slightest reserve will grieve Him to the heart. He spared not Himself, and how can you spare yourself? For your sake He poured out in a lavish abandonment all that He had, and for His sake you must pour out all that you have, without stint or measure.

Hannah Whitall Smith

Love thy neighbor as thyself.

Leviticus 19:18

Don't ever let me get so busy, Lord, that I forget to hold out the right hand of fellowship—to those I know and love, and to those I ought to know and love.

Dale Evans Rogers

See that ye love one another with a pure heart fervently.

I Peter 1:22

I ROSE TO BROTHER ALL

When I once prayed, "Our Father,"
My tears I could not hide.
That day, for the first time
I saw what it implied.
In theory I'd known all
Were sons of God above,
But I saw clearly then
We're brothers born of love.
I then began to live
By faith I'd long professed
And rose to brother all
Whom Jesus died to bless.

Perry Tanksley

Of all the gifts God offers His children, love is the greatest. Of all the fruits of the Holy Spirit, love is the first.

The Bible declares that we who follow Christ should be just as much in love with each other as God was in love with us when He sent His Son to die on the cross. The Bible says that the moment we come to Christ He gives us supernatural love, and that that love is shed abroad in our hearts by the Holy Spirit. The greatest demonstration of the fact that we are Christians is that we love one another. If you learn this secret of God early in your Christian experience, you will have gone a long way toward a mature, happy Christian life.

Billy Graham

NO EAST OR WEST

In Christ there is no East or West,
   In Him no South or North,
But one great Fellowship of Love
   Throughout the whole wide earth.

In Him shall true hearts everywhere
   Their high communion find.
His service is the golden cord
   Close-binding all mankind.

Join hands then, Brothers of the Faith,
   Whate'er your race may be!—
Who serves my Father as a son
   Is surely kin to me.

In Christ now meet both East and West,
   In Him meet South and North,
All Christly souls are one in Him,
   Throughout the whole wide earth.

John Oxenham

VIII. Divine

"... He's everywhere I go ..."
Dee Gaskin

FOOTPRINTS IN THE SAND

One night I had a dream—I dreamed I was walking along the beach with the Lord and across the sky flashed scenes from my life. For each scene I noticed two sets of footprints in the sand, one belonged to me and the other to the Lord. When the last scene of my life flashed before us, I looked back at the footprints in the sand. I noticed that many times along the path of my life there was only one set of footprints. I also noticed that it happened at the very lowest and saddest times in my life. This really bothered me and I questioned the Lord about it.

"Lord, you said that once I decided to follow You, You would walk with me all the way. But I have noticed that during the most troublesome times in my life there is only one set of footprints. I don't understand why in times when I need You most, You should leave me."

The Lord replied, "My precious, precious child, I love you and I would never, never leave you during your times of trials and suffering. When you see only one set of footprints, it was then I carried you."

Author unknown

HE'S EVERYWHERE I GO

The smallest flower, the tallest trees,
The softest breezes that blow.
His gentle hand has made all these;
He's everywhere I go.

His feet have trod the mountains high,
And walked the valleys low.
Still He's concerned for such as I;
He's everywhere I go.

He speaks and makes the lightning flash;
The sky His hands control.
All heav'n and earth obey His voice;
He's everywhere I go.

And then one day He spoke to me,
And, oh, I love Him so.
My destiny is in His hands;
He's everywhere I go.

Dee Gaskin

Love cannot be forced, love cannot be coaxed and teased. It comes
out of Heaven, unasked and un-
sought.

Pearl Buck

Agape love, unconditional love, affirming love—there it was, nailed to the cross and praying a prayer of forgiveness! The world can never understand that love until it experiences that love, because that love is not native to mankind. Human love has its limits. Go beyond them, and our love is all over: "We are friends to the bitter end, but this is the bitter end." Not so with Christ. He loved us to the end.

Louis H. Evans, Jr.

THE SHEPHERD OF SPRING

I saw the dawn in rosy hue
Break o'er the East in great ado.
I heard a robin sweetly sing
Its song of praise to welcome Spring.
I saw a blooming apple tree,
All robed in white, entice the bee.
I saw a fleecy cloud float by—
Majestic—proud, across the sky,
I looked beyond the hills around,
And there my tender Shepherd found.
Not only on the birds and flowers,
But on me too, His love He showers.

Clara Joder

I LOVE YOU, LORD

I love you, Lord, not doubtingly, but with absolute certainty. Your Word beat upon my heart until I fell in love with you, and now the universe and everything in it tells me to love you, and tells the same thing to us all, so that we are without excuse.

And what do I love when I love you? Not physical beauty, or the grandeur of our existence in time, or the radiance of light that pleases the eye, or the sweet melody of old familiar songs, or the fragrance of flowers and ointments and spices, or the taste of manna or honey, or the arms we like to use to clasp each other. None of these do I love when I love my God. Yet there is a kind of light, and a kind of embracing, when I love my God. They are the kind of light and sound and odor and food and love that affect the senses of my inner man. There is another dimension of life in which my soul reflects a light that space itself cannot contain. It hears melodies that never fade with time. It inhales lovely scents that are not blown away by the wind. It eats without diminishing or consuming the supply. It never gets separated from the embrace of God and never gets tired of it. That is what I love when I love my God. . . . I came to love you late, O Beauty so ancient and so new; I came to love you late. You were within me and I was outside, where I rushed about wildly searching for you like some monster loose in your beautiful world. You were with me but I was not with you. You called me, you shouted to me, you broke past my deafness. You bathed me in your light, you wrapped me in your splendor, you sent my blindness reeling. You gave out such a delightful fragrance, and I drew it in and came breathing hard after you. I tasted, and it made me hunger and thirst; you touched me, and I burned to know your peace.

All my hopes are in your great mercy and nowhere else. So give what you command, and command what you will. It is your order that we should practice self-control; the man who insists on loving something besides you does not really love you as he should, unless he loves it because of you. O Love that always burns and is never extinguished! O Love that is my God, set me afire!

St. Augustine
Translated by Sherwood E. Wirt

I know not where His islands lift
Their fronded palms in air;
I only know I cannot drift
Beyond His love and care.

John Greenleaf Whittier

PROOF OF GOD'S LOVE

Jesus was born nearly two thousand years ago, was crucified at about the age of thirty-three, and was buried. In three days He was up and living again, visiting and talking with His friends for a few weeks. Then He left them, and no one has seen His physical body since.

Since that happened, men have sought to understand the true meaning of it all. Great numbers have believed that Jesus was God—that the great God who made the earth came and walked on it for a time, and in doing so left a true picture of Himself.

The record of Jesus' life on earth is the only real proof of God's love and compassion. You cannot find such a picture of God in nature. True, there are beautiful flowers, majestic mountain peaks, and gentle rains from heaven. But there are also fierce storms, the withering heat of the sun, and the dread disease of cancer.

But we can understand this God who came to earth "to seek and to save that which was lost" (Luke 19:10). He came on a mission, and to accomplish it He gave Himself as a ransom for the sins and shortcomings of mankind. The cross will forever stand as our supreme evidence of a loving, suffering, forgiving God.

Charles L. Allen

Man cannot comprehend Infinity. Yet the crumb of our pity comes from the whole loaf of God's compassion. The milk of human kindness comes from the dairies of God's love.

Peter Marshall

FULFILLMENT

Apple blossoms bursting wide now beautify the tree
And make a Springtime picture that is beautiful
    to see . . .
Oh, fragrant lovely blossoms, you'll make a bright
    bouquet
If I but break your branches from the apple tree
    today . . .
But if I break your branches and make your beauty
    mine,
You'll bear no fruit in season when severed from the
    vine . . .
And when we cut ourselves away from guidance that's
    divine,
Our lives will be as fruitless as the branch without the
    vine . . .
For as the flowering branches depend upon the tree
To nourish and fulfill them till they reach futurity,
We too must be dependent on our Father up above,
For we are but the *branches* and He's *the tree of love*.

Helen Steiner Rice

WHAT IS IT THAT I LOVE?

I love to rise at break of morn,
　And wander o'er the fertile plains,
When warblers sweet, proclaim the dawn,
　And fill the air with joyful strains.

I love to view the limpid stream,
　As it meanders gently by,
When sunset with a lingering beam,
　And golden tinge, illumes the sky.

I love the balmy air of eve,
　With dewy tears and zephyr sighs;
It doth the ruffled wind relieve,
　And soothes the spirit ere it flies.

I love the glorious orb of day,
　That gives a sunshine to the heart,
With radiance, gilds life's dreary way,
　And sheds on all an equal part.

I love the bud and blooming rose
　Whose grace and fragrance give delight;
The violet that humbly grows,
　That wins the sense and charms the sight.

I love o'er all fair Nature's Sire,
　Who made the earth, the sea, the sky,
The Architect whom all admire,
　The God Supreme who dwells on high.

Author unknown

Last year I spent a long time in the hospital, and while I am now coming back to my office for a few hours each day when it is possible, it is still very difficult to get adjusted to my new, limited life-style, for it is much more difficult than I ever expected.

I am so aware that there is so much to do in God's vineyard and so little time to do it in. But I'm sure God is restraining me for a purpose, and He never makes mistakes. I think it is God's will that sometimes our minds seem frozen and life stands still . . . and there comes a time we must slacken our pace and accept the fact "we can't run every race!"

Then, too, I think God only takes away our comforts and privileges to make us better Christians, and I personally know that I could never have known God nor loved Him as much without this soul-enlightening touch! Each limitation brings me closer to the greatness and the goodness of God.

I really never knew what tears were, until I had shed some myself, for how can we tell when people's hearts are crying, when our hearts have never wept? And it is so true that the greatest gifts we can give to one another are the gifts of love and understanding.

Helen Steiner Rice

NECESSITY TO UNDERSTAND GOD AS LOVE

If then any child of the Father finds that he is afraid before Him, that the thought of God is a discomfort to him, or even a terror, let him make haste—let him not linger to put on any garment, but rush at once in his nakedness, a true child, for shelter from his own evil and God's terror, into the salvation of the Father's arms.

George Macdonald

ADORATION

I love my God, but with no love of mine,
For I have none to give;
I love Thee, Lord, but all that love is Thine,
For by Thy life I live.
I am as nothing and rejoice to be
Emptied and lost and swallowed up in Thee.

Madame Guyon

HE UNDERSTANDS

There is no circumstance in your life where God will not stand with you and help you, no matter what it is. He understands all your troubles, all your frustrations and disappointments. He understands your weaknesses. He loves you.

Recently my wife and I rode with a taxi driver who proved to be a very interesting man. His name on the license was Dutch and I asked if he was from Europe.

"Yes," he said, "from Rotterdam."

"Well," I replied, "I happen to be minister of the old Dutch Reformed Church in New York."

"Oh," he commented in surprise, "then you're Dr. Peale."

"Yes, sir," I said. . . .

As we drove along he asked, "Have you time to let me tell you a little story? It is about the time I met God, and it shows how good God is. I have great faith, sir, and I know that I can never get outside the care and love of God.

"It was close to the end of the war and I was a little boy. Our country had been ravaged. The conquerors had been driven out, but we were left absolutely destitute. We had ration stamps, but they weren't any good, for we had no food at all. There was no food in the warehouses or in the stores or in the country districts. Holland had been swept clean of foodstuffs.

"We were reduced to eating beets out of the fields and it was a kind of beet that is dangerous to eat without long cooking—and even then if you don't accompany it with other food the chemical reaction will bloat and distend the stomach. People have been known to die from the chemical which they absorbed from an overdose." He continued, "You know how beautiful Holland tulips are? We dug the bulbs out of the ground and ate them. That was all we had. We were desperate.

"Then a notice from our pastor went around, telling us that there would be a meeting in the church; that, since we were reduced to the final circumstances, we would have a meeting and pray to God and tell Him we are His children and ask Him to feed us. It was the only hope we had. The big church was packed; two thousand people were present. There was no sermon. We prayed for an hour or two. The pastor prayed. People prayed aloud all over the church. We sat there herded together, praying to God.

"I was only a little boy, but all of a sudden I became aware that God was right there and I was almost frightened. I could feel Him in my heart. I knew that He was present and I knew that He was going to take care of us poor starving people.

"Then we sang one of those old Dutch hymns of faith and we went out to the streets and to our homes; and with gnawing, empty stomach I fell asleep. Early the next morning we were awakened by the roar of a great armada of airplanes over Rotterdam, filling the avenues with fine food. And we ate. And we were saved."

He glanced back at us from the driver's seat as he said, "As long as I live I will believe that God heard those prayers, and out of His great heart of love He fed his children."

And so do I believe it.

Norman Vincent Peale

I SOUGHT THE LORD

I sought the Lord, and afterward I knew
He moved my soul to seek Him, seeking me;
It was not I that found, O Saviour true,
No, I was found of Thee.

Thou didst reach forth Thy hand and mine enfold;
I walked and sank not on the storm-vexed sea,—
'Twas not so much that I on Thee took hold,
As Thou, dear Lord, on me.

I find, I walk, I love, but, O the whole
Of love is but my answer, Lord, to Thee:
For Thou wert long beforehand with my soul,
Always Thou lovedst me.

Author unknown

The glory of love is brightest
When the glory of self is dim,
And they have the most constrained me
Who most have pointed to Him.
They have held me, stirred me, swayed me,
I have hung on their very word,
Till I fain would get up and follow
Not them, not them, but my Lord.

Author unknown

SOMEBODY CARES

Somebody cares and always will,
The world forgets but God loves you still,
You cannot go beyond His Love
No matter what you're guilty of—
For God forgives until the end,
He is your faithful, loyal friend,
And though you try to hide your face
There is no shelter any place
That can escape His watchful eye,
For on the earth and in the sky
He's ever present and *always there*
To take you in His tender care
And bind the wounds and mend the breaks
When all the world around forsakes . . .
Somebody cares and *loves you still*
And *God* is *the Someone who always will.*

Helen Steiner Rice

Love is the lesson which the
Lord us taught.

Edmund Spenser

GOD IS LOVE

God is LOVE; his mercy brightens
  All the path in which we rove;
Bliss he wakes and woe he lightens;
  God is wisdom, God is love.

Chance and change are busy ever;
  Man decays, and ages move;
But his mercy waneth never;
  God is wisdom, God is love.

E'en the hour that darkest seemeth,
  Will his changeless goodness prove;
From the gloom his brightness streameth,
  God is wisdom, God is love.

He with earthly cares entwineth
  Hope and comfort from above;
Everywhere his glory shineth;
  God is wisdom, God is love.

John Bowring

When God loves, he only desires
to be loved, knowing that love will
render all those who love Him
happy.

St. Bernard

"... BUT HE DID"

God's love is seen in many ways. It is seen first of all in God's creation of this wonderful world in which we live. God did not have to make the heavens vast and beautiful—but He did. God did not have to make the blazing color of the autumn leaves or the quiet music of a mountain stream—but He did. God did not even have to create us with the ability to appreciate the beauty of His creation—but He did, because He loves us. "Every good gift and every perfect gift is from above, and cometh down from the Father of lights with whom there is no variableness, neither shadow of turning" (James 1:17).

Billy Graham

You will ask me questions how a man can give himself to that which he has no feeling of, especially when it relates to an Object which he does not see, nor never had acquaintance with? Sir, every day of your life you love things you do not see. Do you see for instance the wisdom of your friend? Do you see his sincerity, his disinterestedness, his virtue? You cannot see those objects with the eyes of the body, yet you prize and value them, and love them in that degree that you prefer them in your friend to riches, and outward beauty, and to everything that strikes the eye. Love then the wisdom and supreme goodness of God, as you love the wisdom and imperfect goodness of your friend.

François Fénelon

One day I was sitting at my desk when our four-year-old walked through the room trying to thread a needle. If you have never witnessed a small child threading a needle, or attempting to do so, you are in for one of life's great frustrating experiences. The end of the thread was blunt and frazzled, and the needle in her other hand was turned sideways and unsteady in her grasp. My inclination was to snatch it away from her and do it myself. Watching her miss the target over and over again was like listening to a musical number with a dissonant ending; you want to rush to the piano and play the last chord so your soul might rest in peace.

As I watched her, I started to think about the number of times God must want to interrupt what I'm doing and do it Himself. But He is patient. I decided to let her keep trying. Finally, she said, "Daddy, would you do it for me?" I exhaled with satisfaction and relief, took the needle and thread, wet and twisted the thread, inserted it through the needle's eye, and returned it to her. She thanked me and proceeded to play.

Sometimes the Lord lets us get to the end of our rope on a project or ambition because He loves us too much to interfere. If He were to intervene, we would never learn. But once I have tried and failed, and then give it to Him, I know the next time to trust Him with it from the start. God's love is patient, and His patience with me allows me to discover for myself that I can trust Him completely.

Peter Gilquist

I remember one October night visiting a friend who was lying very sick. There was a full moon that night; and as I walked down the village street on my sad mission I felt the silvery beauty of it quiet my heart. The world lay lustrous. There was no scrawny bush nor ugly clod that was not transfigured in that glory. A little breeze over the brimming salt tide brought aromatic marshy odours. It seemed to me that some power was trying to make beauty take away my sadness. I found my friend not less aware than I was of the beauty of the night. He could look from his window and see the argent glamour of it all: how it flooded the gleaming tide with celestial lights; how it ran long white lances through the swarthy cedars; how it tinged with soft radiance the locusts and the mimosas. He felt the breeze too, and delighted in the odours that it brought of the happy world beyond his window. To my surprise, although he was very ill, he greeted me with a strangely elevated calmness and joy.

"I have been," he said, "in many waters, and they are still deep all about me. But God has been with me too. He has not failed me in my distress. Who but He could send this moonlight and this mocking bird singing. He brought them to me, and I think they bring Him near."

As I sat beside him, a mocking bird began to sing in the moonlight, chanting divinely. I know the song reached our spirits. On the table by the bed were all the necessities for a sick man; but he had small comfort from them. But the moonlight, and the hale fragrances, and the wild song of the bird—these brought peace to his heart.

Long afterward he said to me, "Do you remember that night? I thought it would be my last. But from the time the birdsong came through that window I felt that I would get well. I don't talk much about these things, but I felt that all that beauty and peace were really the love of God. I guess He does not love us with words: He loves us by giving us everything we need—in every way."

It must be as he said.

Archibald Rutledge

Index of Authors

Index of Titles

Index of First Lines

It happens in almost every house, 34
It is my joy in life to find, 33
It's no trick at all, 29

Jesus was born, 89

Kindness is a language, 26
Kind words toward those you daily meet, 26

Last eve I walked a certain street, 71
Last year I spent a long time in the hospital, 92
Let us never forget that the love of God, 15
Love cannot be forced, 85
Love communicates an immense value, 68
Love is not blind. Love has 20/20 spiritual vision, 42
Love is the joyous conflict, 54
Love is the lesson, 97
Love seeks not limits, 76
Love thy neighbor, 79
Love vaunteth not itself, is not puffed up, 74

Man cannot comprehend Infinity, 90
Most of my real friends, 27
My heart's in the Highlands, my heart is not here, 55

Not what we give, but what we share, 26
Now that I am seventy, 17

Of all the gifts God offers, 81
Of all the music, 20
Ofttimes across the room you come, 58
One day I was sitting at my desk, 100
One night I had a dream, 84
One of the most beautiful qualities, 34

Preserve sacredly the privacies of your own house, 56

See that ye love one another, 80